TheEmptyChair

Also by the Authors

Getting to the Other Side of Grief: Overcoming the Loss of a Spouse

TheEmptyChair

HANDLING GRIEF on HOLIDAYS and SPECIAL OCCASIONS

SUSAN J. ZONNEBELT-SMEENGE, R.N., ED.D.
AND ROBERT C. DE VRIES, D.MIN., PH.D.

Baker Books

A Division of Baker Book House Co
Grand Rapids, Michigan 49516

Published by Baker Books
a division of Baker Publishing Group
P.O. Box 6287, Grand Rapids, MI 49516-6287
www.bakerbooks.com

Printed in the United States of America

Library of Congress Cataloging-in-Publication Data
Zonnebelt-Smeenge, Susan J., 1948–
    The empty chair : handling grief on holidays and special
occasions / Susan J. Zonnebelt-Smeenge and Robert C. De Vries.
      p.   cm.
    Includes bibliographical references.
    ISBN 10: 0-8010-6377-9 (paper)
    ISBN 978-0-8010-6377-0 (paper)
    1. Bereavement—Religious aspects—Christianity. 2. Grief—
Religious aspects—Christianity. 3. Loss (Psychology) I. De Vries,
Robert C., 1942– II. Title.
BV4905.3.Z66—2001
248.8'66—dc21   2001025316

Scripture quotations are from the HOLY BIBLE, NEW INTERNATIONAL VERSION®. NIV®. Copyright © 1973, 1978, 1984 by International Bible Society. Used by permission of Zondervan. All rights reserved.

15 16   17 16 15

Dedicated with particular appreciation to
William G. and Norma J. Zonnebelt,
wise and loving parents
who have provided continual support
and encouragement
in our writing and speaking on grief issues

Joined on our journey by our children,
Sarah, Brian, Christy, and Carrie,
as we continue to blend our families

*Grief, like the aftermath of a forest fire,
is a process of recovery. Dealing effectively
with the holidays while experiencing
the pain of loss through death
necessitates some extra care and attention.
Join us on a journey exploring both
the pain and eventual joy of rebirth.*

Contents

Preface

What we have once enjoyed we can never lose.

All that we love deeply becomes a part of us.

Helen Keller

BOTH CHAR AND RICK DIED in the month of October. They were our beloved spouses. We experienced the first holidays soon after the death of our partners. First came Thanksgiving, then Christmas, then Easter, with birthdays, anniversaries, and new seasons intermingled. They were difficult. Bob actually set a place at the table for Char at a holiday gathering for friends only to realize his mistake as the guests took their seats. The extra chair remained empty.

Susan wanted to boycott Christmas the first year but decided she could make it through if she and her daughter, Sarah, planned some specific ways to remember Rick while still attempting to celebrate the holidays. To pay tribute to his memory, they lit a ceremonial candle and looked at family pictures together.

For many people, grief at the holidays is an oxymoron. Holidays are supposed to be happy, fun, joyful, overflowing with bonds of love. Grief casts a painful, somber, dark shadow over the holidays, shrouding the happy memories of past celebrations.

We grieve because we loved. We formed an intense attachment to another person. We became vulnerable, letting the other person deep into our life in intimate ways. Attachments, connections, once the glue that held our life together, have now been broken by death. We yearn to have our loved one close to us again.

We grieve not only for the person who died but for the life we lived with that person. We grieve over the loss of someone who functioned in important ways in our life, who was a companion, who shared the same living space. We remember hugging each other, taking walks or eating meals together, and sharing rich holiday traditions.

Now, that part of who you were together is dead. Your own identity is changing. With respect to that person, you are no longer a spouse, child, sibling, parent, or important friend. You may experience the pain of these changes especially during the holidays.

Holidays are special times of the year when we are drawn to remember those significant people who have died, even if the death occurred several years ago and the memories are pleasant and no longer filled with pain. This book, however, is written particularly for those who have experienced a loss recently and who are still in the pain of their grief. The book is the result of a growing conviction that grieving people are eager to receive support and affirmation during the tough early years following the death of a loved one. This support and affirmation is especially needed during holidays and other special times.

We did not write this book for one specific holiday. Obviously, Christmas is a major holiday that holds a particularly difficult challenge for a bereaved person. Other holidays, however, can be just as difficult, as can be birthdays, anniversaries, or other special days within a family or marriage.

Following the deaths of our first spouses, we (Susan, a registered nurse and licensed clinical psychologist, and Bob, an ordained minister and seminary professor) wrote the book *Getting to the Other Side of Grief: Overcoming the Loss of a Spouse.*[1] We wrote this new book specifically about grief and the holidays because many bereaved people often express the need for a specific resource for dealing with traditionally special occasions.

We are committed to the premise that full resolution of grief is possible through a combination of time and intentional grief work. By resolution we mean that a bereaved person can arrive at a point in life where the emotional pain of the death no longer negatively affects his or her life. Of course, even after reaching a satisfying resolution of grief, the bereaved will likely encounter infrequent "firsts" such as a graduation, wedding, and so on that he or she will need to face, but those are time specific and do not need to hinder a person from moving into a full and satisfying new phase in life. The bereaved can live with the sense of being finished with grieving, having addressed everything he or she is aware of that can be dealt with at the present moment.

Using our professions, life experiences, and beliefs, we integrate in this book a sound mental health perspective with a spiritual foundation. As Christians, we found strength through our faith in God. We believe that regardless of one's faith perspective, the spiritual component of a person's life, in which the deeper issues and meaning of life are considered, needs to be addressed by the bereaved to resolve grief fully.

At the same time, however, one's faith must not overshadow the need to approach grief from the perspective of sound mental health. How a person deals with his or her emotions, manages the pain of a significant loss, rebuilds a healthy understanding of himself or herself in the context of this loss, and develops a renewed lifestyle is helped by following healthy mental health practices. In this book the spiritual aspects and the mental health perspectives are treated separately so they can be read individually or in coordination with each other.

Each section is divided into three parts. The first part invites you into the journey through reflecting on your personal experiences. Next, you will find specific suggestions from a sound mental health perspective on how to manage your grief during the holidays or on special occasions. The third part contains a Christian meditation and prayer on the issues under consideration.

While this book deals with the very difficult subject of grief, especially in the context of various holidays and other special occasions, the book is also meant to be reflective and celebrative. The more one experiences life, the more one is able to understand that sometimes the choice is not between joy or sorrow, pain or pleasure. The challenge is to find victory in the middle of the battle, see beauty in the context of despair, or experience joy in the middle of one's pain—and to learn from the experience by constructively reflecting on it.

If you are reading this as a bereaved person, the holidays will never again be exactly the same for you. With the death of a loved one, things change. That does not mean, however, that you will never again be able to join in the celebration or experience the fullness and richness of the holiday. On the contrary, when managed in a healthy way, life for those who have gone through the grieving process can be as full and rich as before (or even more so). Appreciation for smaller things is enhanced; priorities change; things that formerly caused great concern, worry, or anxiety fade into insignificance. Those who have journeyed to the other side of grief will remember the pain and hardship of losing someone, but they can also find a new sense of joy that will become a very special part of future holidays.

To you, the reader, we dedicate this book in the hope that you will find peace in your pain, hope in your hurts, and joy on your journey through grief.

S. Zonnebelt-Smeenge
R. De Vries

The Firestorm

*The challenge of
the firestorm is
to accept its presence.
The devastation is real.
You cannot deny it—
not for very long.*

DEATH IS NEVER IN SEASON. The end of someone's life is never "on time." Very few people die when they or their loved ones want them to—it's either too early or too late, and usually too early. Among the many connections we may make with the timing of a loved one's death, holidays frequently seem to serve as markers of the event.

15

When your loved one died, you may have automatically connected the death to the nearest holiday. Even if that did not happen, the "first" holidays are often an offensive reminder of the death. For most people, "firsts" simply mean the first time they experience a holiday, anniversary, birthday, or other special occasion rich with memory and tradition *without* their loved one.

Some bereaved people may actually experience the emotions of "first" holidays (or other special days) during the second or subsequent years of their grief because of their initial shock, numbness, or tendency to deflect their grief during the first year following the death.

Holidays are, for most people, special times of the year. They come with the regularity of the calendar. We look forward to them, wanting to make each one special and significant. They typically are times away from the pressure of daily work, times for families and friends to gather together, times for reflection and celebration. Thanksgiving Day turkey, a Christmas tree, a Passover meal, an Easter ham, and fireworks on the Fourth of July tend to raise us above the humdrum of life in order to renew and revive. But the holidays will be different for you this year. Grief has likely ripped from you the uncompromised joy and celebration. The firestorm has hit.

Firestorm!

That is what death is like. And the fuel of that fire are the feelings associated with holidays.

Grief is tough enough, but when Christmas comes (or Easter, an anniversary, a birthday, or any other special day), grief becomes all the more difficult. After all, this is supposed to be a happy, joyous time. Grief is the antithesis of joy and is associated with emotions of sadness, emptiness, and loneliness. And now add to your list of "special days" the anniversary date of your loved one's death.

Firestorm!

Remember what happened at Yellowstone National Park a number of years ago? Fire raged with terrifying fury through acres of verdant forest and field. The lush green, heavily wooded mountainsides were ravaged and blackened. Green and gold turned to blackened ash. Deer, bear, and elk had nowhere to hide. Nothing was left standing in the fire's wake. When the fire finally subsided, the only thing that remained was charred black earth with no apparent life, no apparent beauty, no apparent hope. How could this barren ground ever support life again?

Death, like a fire, devastates, destroys. Death seems to leave nothing but ashes in its wake. Landmarks are destroyed. A sense of hopelessness overwhelms. We are not certain whether we can find our bearings again. How will we ever navigate this darkness?

Death, like a forest fire, leaves ashes—ashes of loneliness in the absence of a loved one.

Who died? Over whom do you grieve?

Was it your *spouse,* your life's partner? Your spouse was likely the one with whom you shared your emotional, sexual, social, and spiritual life. With this soul mate you forged your life's dreams, ambitions, and plans. Now you face a solo journey, complicated all the more if your marriage had been stormy or if you have dependent children at home. This holiday can be the time for you to name the pain, to celebrate the memory, and to search the landscape for signs of new life.

Perhaps at this season of the year you grieve the death of your *parent.* The comforting presence of the older generation has been snatched away. The hub, the one who served as an intricate part of your family structure, the one who was instrumental in organizing family gatherings, has died. Your parent, the one who is supposed to believe in you and be a source of unconditional love and acceptance, is gone. This parent is no longer available to consult on important questions as you age. You can no longer escape a sense of your own mortality, for the flesh and blood that brought you into this world has now been taken from this world. Mother's Day and Father's Day will necessarily be altered without your parent. You are now a part of the "oldest" generation—the next in line. This holiday can be the time for you to name the pain, to celebrate the memory, and to search the landscape for signs of new life.

The death of a *child* makes holidays difficult. Society judges such a death as the most unanticipated—the most out of order. In our culture children often occupy a prominent place in the family. They are our link to the future, for they will carry in their hands and hearts the generational torch after we die. This child was to be a significant part of your future, and with his or her death, part of your future died. Perhaps the death was a miscarriage or occurred at the time of delivery. How you yearned to nurture that little life into someone significant, important, loving, and kind! Or your child may have died as an adolescent or adult. In any case, your hopes and dreams for what might have been with this child have been destroyed. So now, on this holiday, you are called to name the pain, to celebrate the memory, and to search the landscape for signs of new life.

A *sister* or *brother* may have died—a comrade in blood. This was the one you teased and with whom you fought, yet you were also bonded with a strong sense of family loyalty. Siblings understand the nature of their shared environment, growing up together. But now the birth order may have changed—you have become the oldest, or maybe the only. Family reunions will forever be different. Family structures will change. Your family is now smaller—one less place setting for the holiday dinner, one less chair at the table. This important person is no longer here. There is now one less person to help with family decisions or plans, one less person to help care for aging parents. And so the holiday forces you to name the pain, to celebrate the memory, and to search the landscape for signs of new life.

The challenge of the firestorm is to accept its presence. The devastation is real. You cannot deny it—not for very long. Holidays seem to intensify the pain and add another layer to one's grief. The special days fall short of what they are imagined to be. Death has removed a significant person from your life. A meaningful relationship has vanished like the morning mist. In the middle of your celebration, you are reminded how closely attached you were to your deceased loved one. Memories of other important people who have preceded you in death may also flood over you.

The firestorm has blown across the prairie of your life. A holiday celebration makes you face the reality of death all the more directly. It may be difficult to say the words *dead* or *died*. They refuse to be shaped by your tongue. Yet in the middle of the traditions of food, family, and friends—and all the activities associated with holidays and other special days—you have an empty chair, a place once filled by that special person, a reminder of the loss.

The loneliness and deep pain threaten to engulf you. Your heart and soul feel burned to the core.

Firestorm!

A c t i o n

Healthy Behaviors

In your journey to the other side of grief, work toward accepting the reality of the death that has occurred. Death seems at one and the same time both real and unreal. How often do you say to yourself, *But this can't be happening to me!* But the death did happen.

Here are some things you can do to better prepare yourself to deal with the upcoming "firsts" of grieving.

- Take care of yourself physically. Holidays can be physically draining, especially if this is your first experience with a holiday since the death of your loved one. Respect your mind and your body. The acronym DEER[1] (drink, eat, exercise, rest) may help you stay focused on taking care of yourself. Holidays take enough energy by themselves without the additional gut-wrenching pain of a death. Failing to take care of yourself physically will only add to your fatigue and frustration.

- Think back to how you celebrated the holidays. What was your role in the celebration? How might that be different now that your loved one has died? Begin to consider how you might want to handle your traditional ways of celebrating this day following your beloved person's death. If you have children (particularly dependent children) or others to consider when deciding how to celebrate the holiday, listen to what is important to them. Then see if you can incorporate their hopes or wishes into the celebration without compromising what you need.

- This year you may merely try to survive the holidays—to get through them. That is okay, especially when you remember that the holidays come every year. You can skip them once (or twice) with the confidence that as you move through your grief you will have more energy to deal with the holidays the next time around.

- Death puts things into perspective. Since the death of your loved one, many of the routine things that previously concerned you may mean almost nothing at all. Some of the festivities and all the hubbub of a particular holiday might seem ridiculous. This is understandable during the grieving process. Reassure yourself that eventually you can come to a new and deeper understanding of each special day.

- Talk with others about the reality that your loved one has died and that therefore your life (and your celebrations) will feel and be different.

- If you accept a holiday invitation to someone's home, give yourself some leeway. Be up front with them when you accept the invitation, letting them know that you will try to participate but that you may well excuse yourself at some point. We suggest that you not host an event during the first year after a death. As a guest you can leave when you want to or even cancel at the last minute. You might also wish to consider making alternative plans that may feel more comfortable, as a back up.

- Remember that a "something" attitude rather than an "all-or-nothing" attitude is a healthy way to approach many issues. You don't have to do everything (or nothing)—you can do *something,* even if it is something small. Perhaps you could pick one activity you traditionally did on this occasion that has special meaning for you. Plan to do that activity again this year, to begin to face the pain of change—to accept the empty chair as part of your celebration.

Reflection

Christian Meditation

I remember my affliction and my wandering,
   the bitterness and the gall.
I well remember them,
   and my soul is downcast within me.
Yet this I call to mind
   and therefore I have hope:
Because of the LORD's great love we are not consumed,
   for his compassions never fail.
They are new every morning;
   great is your faithfulness.
I say to myself, "The LORD is my portion;
   therefore I will wait for him."
The LORD is good to those whose hope is in him,
   to the one who seeks him;
it is good to wait quietly
   for the salvation of the LORD.

Lamentations 3:19–26

C. S. Lewis, a Christian author, once wrote about grief:

No one ever told me that grief felt so much like fear. I am not afraid, but the sensation is like being afraid. The same fluttering stomach, the same restlessness, the yawning. I keep on swallowing.[2]

Emotions can be very confusing. Especially during grief. The emotional component of grief is not just one feeling. It is a composite of many emotions, often including fear, guilt, anger, regret, a sense of abandonment, and the like. And now you face a holiday. Many holidays are highly charged with special religious significance honoring the birth, death, and resurrection of Christ. What are typically joyful emotions associated with these holidays now clash with your grief.

The Bible is filled with many references to grief. The Old Testament talks a great deal about the emotions that likely grip your own soul during this holiday season.

Consider the lamentation of Jeremiah. *Lamentation* literally means "wailing" or "weeping." Jeremiah, who is believed to be the author of this book, bemoans the demise of his nation of Israel. The land has been destroyed. The people have been taken captive. Everything he had built, everything he had planned, and all that which defined his life is now gone. Nothing is left. Death has come to Israel.

Death has also visited your home—likely annihilating for the moment every hope, vision, and dream for the future. "I remember my affliction and my wandering, the bitterness and the gall" (v. 19). How do we make sense of these moments—these utterly destroying events in our lives? Your spouse may have died, or a parent, a child, a sister or brother, a dear friend. And now you face the question, How do I make sense of this?

We suggest that the answer lies in your ability to develop a Christian wait-and-believe attitude. Don't misunderstand this phrase. When Scripture invites us to "wait on the Lord," God isn't suggesting that we take a passive attitude toward our grief. Waiting actually means trusting. Waiting is being patient for the final outcome. Waiting means trusting that *in the end* "God works for the good of those who love him, who have been called according to his purpose" (Rom. 8:28). You can actually use Christian holidays as reminders that the terror of the grave on Good Friday gives way to the victory of the resurrection on Easter. But that calls for a lot of faith, for a solid trust. But the fact that grief is a journey means that we must work while we wait.

Trusting is difficult to do—it is hard work. By trusting we mean depending on someone over whom you have no control to do something for you—like trusting the doctor. Trusting that the check is really in the mail. Trusting that your friend will really call as she promised. Trusting that God will, indeed, be gracious.

Verses 24 and 26 surely indicate that waiting and trusting are the first steps in the healing process. The essence of the Christian faith is learning to trust, especially when you think you simply cannot wait any longer. The hardest times for us were not necessarily the surgeries, or the chemotherapy, or the radiation treatments our spouses received. The hardest times were when it seemed that no one was doing anything, when we simply had to wait. "It is good to wait quietly for the salvation of the LORD" (v. 26).

Isaiah puts this waiting into perspective when he says, "Those who hope in the LORD will renew their strength. They will soar on wings like eagles; they will run and not grow weary, they will walk and not be faint" (Isa. 40:31).

And why wait? Because only those who are truly waiting and trusting can see what is coming. The wait-and-believe attitude means that only those who are truly resting in Christ, truly trusting God, can see what God is doing.

And what will you see? "His compassions never fail. They are new every morning; great is your faithfulness" (vv. 22–23).

Some years ago Kellogg's Corn Flakes challenged television viewers, saying, "Flakes, just ordinary flakes. No nuts, no crunch, no fruit—just flakes. But taste them again—for the first time." A spiritual lesson is embedded in those words.

We can grow so familiar with God's grace that it becomes as bland as corn flakes. We want more—more excitement, more money, more happiness, more status. We don't want just plain flakes.

But then death strikes down that special person. Suddenly everything is turned on its ear. That which had been despised as routine and boring suddenly becomes our only hope.

God's grace is like corn flakes. Usually nothing splashy or grandiose. Grace is just there every morning, faithfully and regularly on your spiritual breakfast table. Flakes—just plain flakes. Like manna—just plain manna. Every morning. You collect just enough for the day. You cannot possess it. You cannot hoard it, or bank it, or invest it. You can merely receive it, fresh and new each day for that day.

In that sense, holidays or other special days are really just "another day" in God's eyes. His grace is new and fresh—every morning. Even for today. Taste his grace again—for the first time.

Prayer

We are not good at trusting, Father. We yearn for control and for power. We want to be strong. How can it be, then, that you would make us weak? How can it be that you would remove from us what little semblance of control we might have? Why does this holiday seem to make my grief harder to bear? Make clear your strength, power, and grace—not just on the occasion of my hurts and grief, but through them. Help me to see each day, either a routine day or a holiday, as a day of grace from you. Help me to wait quietly for your direction. Quiet my confused heart. Make me diligent in doing all that I need to do to get through this grief, and impress on me again that your compassion never fails. Great is your faithfulness. *Amen.*

Sorting through the Ashes

Yet on the side of the mountain where the fire recently raged there are the desolate remains of smoldering ash. . . . This is where you are—with the painful emptiness of the loss of a loved one.

FIRES RAGE THROUGH ACRES OF TIMBERLAND, destroying miles of beautiful forest. The pain of seeing majestic towering tree lines sucked up by flames is heart-wrenching. But fires do not burn forever. They eventually subside, sometimes on their own but most often through the hard work of a fire-fighting force. Ashes

29

remain—often hot for days, slowly cooling in air filled with the acrid smell of charred timber.

Funeral rituals following the death of a loved one are like that. The visitations, memorials, flowers, and casseroles delivered by well-meaning friends and family slowly taper off. The whirlwind gradually comes to a halt. Other people's lives return to normal. Their attention may diminish after a few weeks or months.

Portions of the forest, not touched directly by the fire, return rather quickly to the quiet, balanced, majestic life. Food can be found in rich abundance in places unaffected by the fire. Elk feed as usual by the river bank. Eagles soar overhead. Yet on the side of the mountain where the fire recently raged there are the desolate remains of smoldering ash. Barren. Desolate. No animals. No lush greenery. This is where you are—with the painful emptiness of the loss of a loved one.

Holidays make the feelings of devastation, grief, anxiety, fear, anger, guilt (and a multitude more) all the more pointed. The one who helped decorate the house, prepare a festive meal, and rip open the presents, the one who read the religious rituals or sang in a holiday program is no longer with you. You sense you are on your own now. And it hurts. The empty place is an immense gaping hole. A major tear in your heart seems to be gushing your life's blood. Someone who was an integral part of your life has died. You miss that person and the life you had together.

You probably don't feel at all festive or eager for a holiday to come. You may be looking for an escape, a

Rip Van Winkle sleep. You can do just that by choosing to drastically downsize your celebration or to travel over this holiday. Deciding to move in slow motion won't hurt anything this year. But eventually you will recognize the importance of facing the pain. Give yourself permission to do what is best for you on this special occasion, but know that you cannot avoid the holidays forever.

Maybe this year is the time for you to put holidays in their proper perspective. Most, if not all, of the holidays celebrated in North America came at a great price in the beginning. Christmas, for Christians, is not fully understood without also recognizing the specter of the cross overshadowing it. The Passover in the Jewish community is marked by the death of thousands as the Angel of the Lord "passed over" the houses of the faithful in Israel. Easter is a reminder of the extreme sacrifice of Jesus on the cross. Yet the day is also a symbol of new life, of hope for the future.

Thanksgiving Day is marked by the sacrifice and death of many of the early settlers of America who made the journey for religious freedom but fell victim to disease and storm during the first hard winter in the New World. Memorial Day and the Fourth of July are celebrations rooted in the many lives sacrificed for our freedom.

Holidays have an inherent value and meaning that can be enhanced through the gathering together of loved ones. During this holiday season, in your bereavement, it may be helpful to focus on the underlying meaning of the holiday rather than on some of the activities that were traditional for you and your family.

Holidays are typically emotional times anyway. This year you have experienced a pronounced painful change due to the death of a loved one. We encourage you to experience and express your emotions during this special season or day. You may need to be reminded that emotions do not just go away if you ignore them. If they are not given expression, they are deposited somewhere inside us where, often unannounced, they manifest themselves in unhealthy ways months or years later. Pent-up emotions lie at the root of many physical illnesses, emotional problems, or make future grief situations all the more difficult.

The sights and sounds of the holidays will likely trigger many memories for you—some of which will be happy. But the memories will be marked with sadness and pain, at least from the perspective that these events will no longer happen in the same way.

You may be saying, "I don't want this holiday to come. I just want to avoid it this year. Let's just skip it. Flip the calendar and move into the next month." But there is no way to push the calender ahead. Time moves in a twenty-four-hour sequence, a fact that can be seen as a comfort. It is just one day, you know—with only about eighteen waking hours. Maybe you can encourage yourself with that thought. We can all live through eighteen hours, even if we just wait them out. We also know that facing tough situations can help us move through our pain, and we can move one step closer toward getting to the other side of grief.

Ironically, facing your pain along with the other emotions of grief is healing and can produce growth. So deal with your grief now as best you can. Anticipate and make plans for each holiday or special day. Do what you can to anticipate what otherwise might blindside or overwhelm you. Plan some time to be by yourself so you can grieve and reflect on your memories without the pressure of family or social obligations. Tackle a few things at a time, and don't concern yourself with the rest for now. Leave some activities for another time.

Grief happens, but you can use it to grow.

A c t i o n

Healthy Behaviors

> Your grief journey is an emotional one. Learn to embrace all the emotions associated with the death of your loved one. Some of these emotions may be terribly frightening. Some may even conflict with others. But dealing with the emotions directly will help you get to the other side of grief.

Here are some things you can do to better prepare yourself to deal with the emotions associated with your grief.

- Lower your expectations and the pressures you put on yourself. You do not have to celebrate the holiday in exactly the same way you did before. Even if your loved one had not died, each special day would still differ from the last one. Time alone automatically brings changes to our lives. This holiday you are forced to face a very traumatic change. Give yourself the gift of time. The holiday itself will be only twenty-four hours in length. Plan your day, keeping it simple. Allow yourself time to face the hard reality of your loved one's death (in a manageable dose) if you think you can do so this year. For some of you, celebrating the holiday according to family tradition may be a comforting coping strategy. If it is not, take a break from the holiday this time, making the commitment to yourself that you will face this special day more directly next year.

- Don't keep yourself so busy that you avoid your feelings or distract yourself from the reality that your loved one is no longer alive. Your loved one has died. Many people may expect or want you to deny or avoid your pain. Others may try to influence you to put your grief out of your mind. They may mean well, but perhaps they have little awareness of what grief is like. Remember that feelings just *are*—feelings are okay. Even though people may not want to see you in pain, be true to yourself. It is okay to cry and look sad. The more you face the pain directly the more quickly you will be able to conquer the pain and move on to a full resolution of your grief.

R e f l e c t i o n

Christian Meditation

As the deer pants for streams of water,
    so my soul pants for you, O God.
My soul thirsts for God, for the living God.
    When can I go and meet with God?
My tears have been my food day and night,
    while men say to me all day long,
"Where is your God?" . . .
Why are you downcast, O my soul?
    Why so disturbed within me?
Put your hope in God,
    for I will yet praise him,
    my Savior and my God.

Psalm 42:1–3, 11

Those who sense God's presence in their lives during the "normal times" can also sometimes sense a great gulf between themselves and God during tough times. Death not only separates us from our loved one but can, in some cases, give us the sense that we are also separated from God. That is when we yearn for his presence, for his touch, for some sign of his caring and compassion.

The writers of the above psalm (known as the Sons of Korah) yearned to be close to God, but they also knew how difficult it was to get near God at times. Their soul *pants* for God, their soul *thirsts* for God, all the while hearing others taunt them in a jeering voice saying, "Where is your God?"

Death often throws us into the dark night of the soul, a phrase often used by writers in the Christian tradition to denote those periods in life when we seem far from God. Sometimes we cannot draw near to God because we are simply burned out—emotionally and spiritually. Like a frightened child, we feel abandoned, alone, downcast, and disturbed.

Along with these feelings and the overwhelming emotions of grief, Christians might also feel guilty for feelings of abandonment, anger, frustration, or lack of closeness with God. Somehow we may have come to believe that Christians are supposed to be victorious, happy, powerful, and positive all the time. Somehow we have been led to believe that emotions (especially the "negative ones" such as anger, fear, a sense of abandonment, and the like) really have no place in our faith. When we experience these feelings, we wonder if we have enough faith. Propelled by a sense of guilt, we are at times tempted to think that if only we had prayed harder, God might have spared our loved one. Remember, God doesn't *cause* death; he *allows* it because of our human brokenness.

Emotions are neither good nor bad. Emotions are merely part of our human existence. Even Jesus in his perfect state had emotions, and he was not afraid of expressing them. He wept at the grave of Lazarus, even though he was about to bring him back to life (John 11:35).

You may firmly believe that your loved one is in heaven, enjoying that eternal reward so longed for on this earth. But the fact that he or she is in heaven does not mean you should not cry. If Jesus himself cried over the death of his loved one—whom he would raise back to life—how much more do you think crying is legitimate and permissible for you?

Later, as Christ approached Jerusalem the week before his own death, he cried out: "O Jerusalem, Jerusalem, you who kill the prophets and stone those sent to you, how often I have longed to gather your children together, as a hen gathers her chicks under her wings, but you were not willing" (Matt. 23:37). Disappointment, grief, mourning—they were also part of Jesus' life.

So you yearn for God's presence and power in your life. Perhaps because of the holidays, especially those filled with special religious significance, you may find it even more difficult to worship and draw near to God. Your anger may stand in the way. Or your own regret, a sense of guilt for what you think you could have done, might be the obstacle. Return to Psalm 42. The call is clear: "Put your hope in God, for I will yet praise him, my Savior and my God" (v. 11). The Christian holidays ultimately remind us of the victory of God's grace. He gives us hope.

Hope—that is the key word. Hope is the capacity to see through the darkness of this moment to the returning light of tomorrow. Hope allowed Jesus to see past his own grief over Lazarus's death—even past the terror of his own crucifixion—to see the joy that lay beyond. But he didn't get to the other side by denying his emotions.

We do not grieve as others do because of our hope in God (1 Thess. 4:13). As Christians we *do* grieve, but we have the solid hope and confidence that God will be with us through this horrific experience of grieving. Somehow he will work through this experience to bring good from it. This is the promise of Easter.

We need to consider one other aspect of emotions for a moment. The busier we make ourselves, the more we immerse ourselves in funeral arrangements, legal and financial management, social engagements, and other matters surrounding the death in an attempt to fill the empty spaces, the easier it is for us to avoid our emotions. Solitude allows these emotions to rise to the surface. Perhaps we don't want to feel our grief intensely, so we avoid being alone. But this is precisely when we need to spend some time alone—with ourselves and with God. Take a walk by yourself, sit by a sparkling lake or resonate with the pounding surf, hike in a quiet woods, or crunch through the snow. Such occasions provide the opportunity for reflective solitude. Holidays have a way of usurping time. Reclaim some of it for yourself. The psalmist encourages us to be quiet in the presence of

God: "Be still, and know that I am God; I will be exalted among the nations, I will be exalted in the earth" (Ps. 46:10).

Find a quiet place for yourself this holiday or special day. Know that being alone in God's presence is a healing activity. He is there. You are not alone.

Prayer

Fears and feelings of guilt, regret, or anger often seem to overwhelm us, Father. We want to run, to hide. We are sometimes ashamed to admit that we are so weak, especially in our faith. Why did this death have to occur? Why didn't you hear my prayers? Why do you seem so far away? Help me to have the faith of the psalmists, who were able to express their fears while keeping their faith. Give me confidence that even though I cry and wail, you will still give me hope. Help me to focus on Jesus, believing—and knowing—that he will see me through. *Amen.*

THREE

A Time to Remember

Memories are designed to free you to move out of the night into a new day.

SOMEONE WHO HAD MADE FREQUENT TRIPS to Yellowstone might remember, standing in the center of a scorched field in the heart of the park, what it had been like. He or she might be able to reminisce, to think back to how the lush fields once looked, and be able to sort through a storehouse of memories to recall brighter days.

41

Memories need to be revisited and sorted. Charles Dickens, in his classic tale *A Christmas Carol,* recognized this truth. Scrooge had to relive Christmas past, visit Christmas present, and anticipate Christmas future.

On this holiday or special day, we invite you to journey back to previous years, gather the memories, and begin the sorting process. Remember the anticipation and fun of shopping for just the right gift for the loved one who died. Remember trudging through the snow with that person to cut down the slightly out-of-shape Christmas tree, which, when adorned with glistening lights and favorite ornaments, created a bright, festive atmosphere in your home. Recall the family gathered around the Thanksgiving meal and the table aching under the weight of all the food—laughter and stories filling the room. Revisit a Fourth of July or Labor Day picnic on the shores of a lake, complete with the aroma of grilling burgers and the gleeful sounds of children's voices floating over from the playground.

And remember the other aspects of these holidays or special days—perhaps the tensions that may have risen when you wanted to do something one way and your deceased loved one wanted to do it another way. No two people think exactly alike, so differences were bound to arise. Remember the stress that may have come with the family gatherings. Sometimes the busyness and expectations of a holiday created tensions and potential conflicts in addition to the good times. If conflicts are a part of your memories, accept the fact that these are normal parts of our imperfect personal histories. Work hard to avoid using these memories as an occasion to increase your feelings of guilt.

Memories are designed to free you to move out of the night into a new day. This is the message of the well-known refrain from *Cats,* which encourages you to remember the old days while a new day and life begin.

This holiday or other special day provides you with a challenge and an opportunity. Begin now to sort through your memories. Learn to cherish them. Find a place to store them in your mind and heart. But make sure they are accurate memories. Remember the joy, the fun, the laughter, but also remember the tears, the strained tones, the idiosyncracies that may have annoyed you. Keep those memories in balance. Don't sanctify your memories of your loved one.

Remember the entire orchestra of feelings you had for your loved one. No one is asking you to forget what holidays were like before the death. You could not forget even if you wanted to. Remember it all, and store the memories in such a way that you can retrieve them at will—similar to what you have done with your childhood memories.

At some point as you move through your grief process, you will probably *remember* the pain, but you will no longer experience the painful emotions. The special memories will remain.

A c t i o n

Healthy Behaviors

> Memories are powerful. Your memories of the experiences you shared with your deceased loved one can make the past a significant part of who you are in the present. As you attempt to move to the other side of grief, you will need to learn how to store these memories in your heart and mind in such a way that you can recall them accurately but at the same time no longer feel the emotional pain associated with them.

Here are some things you can do to store the memories in the past so that you can move on in the present.

- Talk about your deceased loved one. Tell a favorite story, give a toast, write a poem, play his or her favorite song, or make a favorite food. Such an act will help you express the importance of the deceased person, and then perhaps you and other family members will be able to move on to appreciate the holiday with an even deeper significance. Talking about the person who died will help you accept the reality of the person's death, express some of the emotions associated with your loss, and revisit your memories of this special person.

- Write a letter to your deceased loved one, recalling several memories you have of the holidays in which this person played an important part. In that letter, write about such things as:

> "When I think of this holiday without you, I feel . . ."
>
> "The thing I will miss most on this special day without you is . . ."
>
> "The things I didn't like about this special day with you were . . ."
>
> "The things that you gave me that were important were . . ."

Perhaps you might even go to the cemetery to read the letter out loud.

- Using photos, make a picture book of the holidays and other special occasions. Or use them to make a video or slide presentation. Find some way to organize your visual memories so that you and your family can use them during the holiday celebration to remember this special person.
- Go through cards, letters, pictures, and other personal memorabilia associated with your relationship with your deceased loved one. Relive the oc-

casions and remember this special person as you review the mementos.

- Ask your friends and family to write down their memories of your deceased love one and collect them in a keepsake book.

R e f l e c t i o n

Christian Meditation

So Joshua called together the twelve men he had appointed from the Israelites, one from each tribe, and said to them, "Go over before the ark of the LORD your God into the middle of the Jordan. Each of you is to take up a stone on his shoulder, according to the number of the tribes of the Israelites, to serve as a sign among you. In the future, when your children ask you, 'What do these stones mean?' tell them that the flow of the Jordan was cut off before the ark of the covenant of the LORD. When it crossed the Jordan, the waters of the Jordan were cut off. These stones are to be a memorial to the people of Israel forever."

Joshua 4:4–7

And when [Christ] had given thanks, he broke it and said, "This is my body, which is for you; do this in remembrance of me."

1 Corinthians 11:24

You can find memorials, statues, and plaques in almost every park in the United States and Canada. Many of them honor war heroes—sculptures of the valiant on horseback, or brave heros with arms folded victoriously across their chests. Who hasn't stood in awe when seeing for the first time the representation of the soldiers raising the flag on Iwo Jima, or when standing face to face with the black granite wall of the Vietnam Memorial, containing thousands of names of war victims engraved deeply in its surface? Many of our memorials are associated with war, with death, with victory, and with memories.

Interesting companions, aren't they: war, death, victory, and memory? We hope the parallel is not lost when you think of the death of your loved one. There was the battle with disease, or your own battle in accepting the fact of the sudden heart attack or accident. Then came the death, the heart-wrenching reality that the physical body of your loved one had ceased breathing.

But for Christians, death is also associated with victory and memories. Seeing the victory may take some time, especially if the death occurred recently. At first you may appropriately cling to the victory your loved one has experienced—that final victory of making the transition from this world to the next, in which there is no more death, pain, or suffering (Rev. 21:4). The apostle Paul's promise is certain:

"Where, O death, is your victory?
     Where, O death, is your sting?"

The sting of death is sin, and the power of sin is the law. But thanks be to God! He gives us the victory through our Lord Jesus Christ.

1 Corinthians 15:55–57

Hopefully you rest in the comfort of knowing that your loved one has experienced his or her own victory, being freed from the brokenness of this world and having entered paradise with God. Your loved one has now completed his or her journey on this earth. After all, is that not the ultimate purpose for us as Christians in this life? So we rejoice for our loved one who is now enjoying the delights and victory of heaven.

However, you are still living in this world. What about your own sense of victory? Many who grieve find that the phrase often used by well-wishers, "Well, at least he is in a better place," does *not* provide the comfort they imagine it might. As a matter of fact, such a comment often produces a negative reaction. Feelings of unworthiness, guilt, or abandonment by God can overwhelm the bereaved person. "Why couldn't it have been me?" "Why does she get to go to heaven, and I have to stay here to deal with this mess?"

So we need to work toward our own sense of victory—victory over the grip of grief itself. An important step in that process is moving from the emptiness and pain that death brings to formulating memories of your loved one. The Bible provides a number of powerful examples of how that works.

The passage from the Book of Joshua, quoted above, takes us back to the time when the nation of Israel fled Egypt after the slaughter of the firstborn Egyptians, while the Angel of the Lord passed over (hence, the Passover) the Israelites. After wandering for forty years in the wilderness, the Israelites crossed the Jordan River into the Promised Land. God wanted the nation to remember the battle in Egypt, the death of the children at the time of the Passover, and the death of their ancestors in the wilderness, but he also wanted them to sense the victory of entering the Promised Land. So he commanded them to build a memorial, a pile of stones, so that they (and all the generations after them) would remember.

One of our greatest fears is that we, or others, will forget. We are afraid that no one will remember our deceased child, parent, sibling, or spouse. Even more so, we are afraid others will expect us to forget. Somehow, they may equate moving on into a full and rich life with forgetting the past.

The Christian holidays of Christmas, Good Friday, and Easter may be painful for you right now. They are painful *because* they serve as an occasion for memories—memories of what your loved one meant in your life, but also memories of God's concern for you and how he has woven a plan for your eternal salvation.

Christmas, for example, is certainly more than decorated trees, songs of snowmen, and hectic shopping and gift giving. Christmas is a time to recall God's great love for us symbolized in the birth of the Christ child.

As you grieve the death of your loved one, use the Christmas holiday to remember God's gift, which is so great that it encompasses all your pain.

The season of Lent can also serve as a memory that can surround your pain. The love that God has for us brought him to the agony of the cross. As you grieve, consider using the Lenten season to remember God's own sacrifice in the death of his Son so that your experience with death is set within the context of God's love and power. Undoubtedly, facing death on the cross was a battle that only Christ could bear. The writer of the Book of Hebrews invites us to "fix our eyes on Jesus, the author and perfecter of our faith, who for the joy set before him endured the cross, scorning its shame, and sat down at the right hand of the throne of God" (Heb. 12:2). In the process of going to the cross, Jesus himself established a memorial— the Lord's Supper, or Eucharist. He wants us to remember our battle with sin and brokenness. He wants us to remember his death. But he also wants us to celebrate his victory for us and to cling to his promise of eternal life. Bread and wine became the symbols of life and peace, of health and wholeness.

Easter is the highlight of the Christian holidays, for it symbolizes most directly Christ's victory over death— death, which is the source of your grief. If you are reading this book during the Easter season, know that Jesus Christ (who also endured death) brings life not just to the deceased but also to those who grieve. We do grieve.

But we grieve with hope. Christ's resurrection is the symbol of the new life you can have even after the death of a loved one as he helps you move through your grief to rebuild your life here on earth.

God does not want us to forget our past. God does not want us to forget the good times, the hard times, the successes, the mistakes. God does not ask that you forget that wonderful, or at times conflictual, relationship. Moving on does not mean forgetting. It means victory. The battle is over for your loved one. Death has come. Now you can experience his or her victory of a new life while constructing memories for yourself of your past life with your loved one.

Whatever holiday or other special day you are presently facing, know that you have the opportunity to begin collecting your memories. The time has come to move the battle and the death into your memories. Creating memories is, by definition, moving an event into the past. Memories are things that have happened. They are no longer present. We can relish remembering them as we choose. They become a part of our historical lifeline. But memories allow us to move on as well.

We may visit memorials periodically. We remember the battles, the deaths, the victories. But we do not live at the memorials. We get back into our car, return home, and take up our life again.

You have visited the grave. Now visit God's grace, a grace that will help you move the events of the death into the realm of treasured memories. And as you do so, you will find that you are free to move on in your life. You are free to make the holidays and other special occasions your own personal celebration, combining memories of the past with new hopes and dreams for the future.

Prayer

We are people of the past, present, and future. Help us, heavenly Father, to keep these time frames in perspective. You have taught us to know the value of the past. Some of the memories you have allowed us to create are happy ones. Others are tragic or sorrowful. Give me the grace to move the death of my loved one into my memory. May the memories find a place of honor in my life, but may I also be able to live fully in the present, which you have given me, and to move into the future with hope and confidence that you are guiding, empowering, and healing me. *Amen.*

Planting the Seeds for New Life

A new beginning is possible, like new life in a charred forest.

REMEMBER THE FIRE? Can you see, again, the charred forest floor blackened and dead? If you visited Yellowstone a few years after the fire, you would have seen the growth, the new greenery, the lush vegetation that had

55

sprung up again. Ecologists know that this form of death in a forest is necessary for new life and growth. This is part of the environmental system. It is the way nature recycles and replenishes itself.

As much as you may have liked "the old way" of your life, death has changed it. The old forest is gone. Your loved one's death has altered the picture of the past landscape. Your life will not be the same again. That speaks to the significance of your deceased loved one. But you can also have a new beginning. After all, your life will go on, and you need to decide *how* that will happen. In some ways, grieving is a solo journey—a journey you eventually need to walk intentionally by yourself.

Out of the devastation, a new chapter—a whole new volume—of your life can emerge. You can begin again. A new beginning is possible, like new life in a charred forest. You may not have anticipated, or wanted, a new beginning. Change is not usually something any of us seek. That is not part of our human nature. We like things to stay the same. Comfortable. Known. We at least want continuity. We want to hold tight to our families, including parents, siblings, and children. As spouses, we want to grow old together. And even after the devastation of death, we will not forget. We remember how it was.

But if you as a bereaved person hang on and continue in your grief, if you never relinquish the pain, if you continue to feel that moving on in your life might be disloyal to the one who died, then you are saying that the one who died is of more importance than you are.

Perhaps you think that Yellowstone, or Yosemite, or the Grand Canyon can never be beautiful again after a fire. It definitely does seem like that for a while. And the same is true following the death of a loved one. But eventually you can feel differently.

C. S. Lewis writes in his book *A Grief Observed,* "There was no sudden striking emotional transition. Like the warming of a room, or the coming of daylight, when we first notice them they have been going on for some time."[1]

Grief is a process. Working through grief is like the gradual coming of daylight. And it will likely occur in small bits and pieces, like puzzle pieces, until eventually all aspects come together to signify healing, and you will no longer be in pain.

In remembering your loved one today, we challenge you also to remember yourself. Yes, you can benefit from taking time to remember your loved one, to construct your memories of him or her. That is a healthy thing to do and a very appropriate way to remind yourself of the meaning that person had in your life. But your loved one died; you didn't. You were and are an individual with your own worth and merit independent of your loved one. Now is the time to identify and reaffirm who you are as a person—a person of much value and worth, even without your loved one who died.

You now have the present to cope with. How are you going to deal with this upcoming holiday or special occasion? Like Scrooge who was invited to assess his Christmas present, can you see what is going on right now? Can you see your family, your friends, your meaningful traditions? Can you see that you are still here, and see that as a gift? Your loved one has died, but you are still here. How do you want to live this holiday season?

There are most likely others in your life who want to give you love and receive your love as well. Don't isolate yourself completely, although time for individual reflection and solitude is helpful and healthy. Perhaps you have dependent children to consider when you plan your holiday or special day. That will add another challenge because grief can be all-encompassing, absorbing, and self-focused. Obviously you may have to consider others on some occasions during this holiday, along with taking care of yourself. Be true to your own inclinations and needs. Grief can be like a juggling act, finding a way to do what you need to do while also considering other people's needs and desires to some extent.

Take time today to say to yourself, "I can move on." The passing of time will change you, whether you like it or not. But you need to decide if you are merely going to allow these things to happen to you or if you are going to take control to redefine yourself—to invest with energy (even gusto as time progresses!) in the next phase of your life.

If you are going to take charge of your life as an individual, you will need to energize yourself and become deliberate about what you need to do. Realize you need to let go. Not, of course, to forget the deceased person.

But you also do not want to keep looking back and hanging on to the past. Remember *and* let go and move on. Like a toddler letting go of the furniture that has steadied his or her gait, you can begin again without hanging on—in order to move toward new horizons and adventures in the life that awaits you.

Hope can rise from the ashes. New life can emerge. You can get through this time of grief to become a stronger, wiser, and more empathic person.

A c t i o n

Healthy Behaviors

As you move through the grief process, you will begin to see yourself as separate emotionally and psychologically from your deceased loved one. That does not mean forgetting. But you do need to discover who you are as a person independent of that prior relationship.

Here are some things you can do to separate your own self from that of your loved one.

- Remember that you can have wonderful memories of your deceased loved one associated with past holidays and other special occasions, but that undoubtedly you enjoyed those days or times for other reasons as well. Your loved one died; you didn't. Try to find something that will give you a renewed view of the day—if only for a portion of the time.

- Make a list of the things you like about each holiday or special day—things that you perhaps enjoyed even before your relationship with the deceased. Identifying these things may rekindle a spark of pleasure as you reemphasize them in your life.

- Make a plan for incorporating into your celebration of this holiday those specific things that you want to include. In other words, develop specific strategies for how you might implement them. When will you do it? How will you do it? With whom will you do it? There is a decided advantage in thinking ahead about what you want that special day to include.

- You now have an additional and most likely difficult "special day," namely, the anniversary date of the death of your loved one. How do you want to remember and honor your relationship with that person on the date of his or her death? You might light a candle, write your loved one a letter, visit the cemetery, reread special greeting cards, or look at pictures. Whatever you do, the anniversary of the death during the first few years will undoubtedly be an occasion for some painful emotions. But it will also provide an excellent opportunity to work toward healing the pain. See the appendix for sample memorial tributes (one for general use, the other from a Christian perspective) that you might use on a holiday or other special occasion.

- Consider doing one or a few of your traditional activities on the holiday or special day that you enjoyed doing with your loved one or as a family. Sing a favorite Christmas carol, recite a favorite toast, poem, or story, dine out or serve a special food. Then make the rest of the holiday or special day the way you individually (and in coordination with any dependent children) want it to be. There is no one right way. You are a unique individual, and there are many different ways for you to grieve as well as celebrate.

R e f l e c t i o n

Christian Meditation

Where can I go from your Spirit?
  Where can I flee from your presence?
If I go up to the heavens, you are there;
  if I make my bed in the depths, you are there.
If I rise on the wings of the dawn,
  if I settle on the far side of the sea,
even there your hand will guide me,
  your right hand will hold me fast.
If I say, "Surely the darkness will hide me
  and the light become night around me,"
even the darkness will not be dark to you;
  the night will shine like the day,
  for darkness is as light to you.
For you created my inmost being;
  you knit me together in my mother's womb.
I praise you because I am fearfully and
    wonderfully made;
  your works are wonderful,
  I know that full well.
My frame was not hidden from you
  when I was made in the secret place.

When I was woven together in the depths of
the earth,
your eyes saw my unformed body.
All the days ordained for me
were written in your book
before one of them came to be.

Psalm 139:7–16

You have loved another person deeply. With his or her death, you are now caught in the grip of grief. In loving the other person, you also received love from him or her. Being loved by someone else helps to validate your own worth. Someone accepts you, depends on you, forgives you, appreciates and values you—you are connected with another.

But that person is now dead. Their love for you is now a memory—a precious memory to be sure, but still a memory. With each passing day, with each new experience, the distance between that memory and your present life becomes greater. Who will love me now? Will I ever have a similar love like that again—whether it be the love of a parent, spouse, child, or sibling?

Instead of looking immediately to other people as a source of love and support, we encourage you to look in two directions: to God and to yourself.

Looking to God is, of course, a natural response for a Christian. But God can at times seem so distant from us in our grief. At those times, grief has a way of making us think that God has left us—we are alone. But Psalm 139 is a powerful reminder that God is everywhere. You can go to the heavens or to the depths of the earth, and you will find God there. Grief can cover you with darkness, but to God, even the darkness is light (v. 12).

Verses 13 and 14 say, "For you [God] created my inmost being; you knit me together in my mother's womb. I praise you because I am fearfully and wonderfully made." Notice the emphasis on you—as an individual. You are the one God made. You are wonderful. You are awe-inspiring. You are created in God's image (Gen. 1:27). Not you in the relationship you have now lost through death. You—alone—before God.

Now, also consider that the New Testament says you are a "new creature," a "new creation" in Christ. "Therefore, if anyone is in Christ, he is a new creation; the old has gone, the new has come!" (2 Cor. 5:17). If God was so intent on creating you individually and purposefully, and if Christ made you a new creation through his sacrifice, does it not follow that God loves you more than any other human possibly could?

Some Christians may be confused about the concept of self-esteem, or feeling good about one's self. Somehow the Christian tradition, perhaps with its emphasis on sin, has left the impression that we are unworthy. Or we have twisted Scripture so that we think being humble means demeaning ourselves, thinking we are nothing. The truth is that God loved you so much that he sent his Son as the Savior of your life for eternity (John 3:16). We suggest you put your own name in that verse, for your life did not end with the death of your loved one. You are still loved by God.

We said earlier that you might look to God and then to yourself. We encourage you to think of the "love connection" this way. If God has loved you so much that he considers you a treasure, and if he wants you to love others ("love your neighbor"), then you must also love yourself ("love your neighbor as yourself") (Luke 10:27). If you cannot love yourself, you will have no love to give others. You cannot give to someone else what you do not have yourself.

A very important part of the grieving process is developing the capacity to say, "I am special." You are a unique creation of God with a special blend of talents, perspectives, emotions, and dreams. There is no one else like you. And even though your loved one has died, you are not dependent on that relationship for your identity.

The change in focus from your deceased loved one to yourself may be a difficult transition for you to make. New Year's Eve and New Year's Day can be especially challenging times for someone grieving the death of a loved one. A spouse will no longer have a partner for the midnight dance and kiss. A child will not have the concerned and loving parent with whom to share New Year's resolutions. On the other hand, the movement from one year to the next may serve as a beneficial point of transition in your grief journey. The new year could well be the time for you to reclaim and redefine your place in life. New Year's is a form of Sabbath—an Old Testament concept and practice in which everyone begins again. The Sabbath is not just a day of the week for rest. The Sabbath concept means a new beginning, a new start. In the Year of Jubilee, the ultimate expression of Sabbath, debts were forgiven, prisoners were freed, and everyone was able to begin life all over again (Leviticus 25).

The time has come for you to separate yourself from the past and turn your face toward your future. The time has come to reinvest in life, to create your own "new year." Join with the apostle Paul in the confidence that "he who began a good work in you will carry it on to completion until the day of Christ Jesus" (Phil. 1:6). This means that you need to "press on" in your journey, confident that everything is under God's control. The psalmist said, "All the days ordained for me were written in your book before one of them came to be" (Ps. 139:16). Your life still has purpose and meaning. That meaning or purpose may not be clear to you yet, or perhaps you are beginning to sense that new opportunities and directions are opening up to you.

Through prophets such as Isaiah, God constantly reminded his chosen people of Israel of his gracious providential care. The Israelite nation went through many difficult times—times of defeat, times of grief. Among the many messages Isaiah brought to Israel was this promise, which is also appropriate for those who grieve:

The Spirit of the Sovereign LORD is on me,
   because the LORD has anointed me
   to preach good news to the poor.
He has sent me to bind up the broken-
      hearted, . . .
to comfort all who mourn, . . .
to bestow on them a crown of beauty
   instead of ashes,
the oil of gladness
   instead of mourning,
and a garment of praise
   instead of a spirit of despair.

Isaiah 61:1–3

God will heal your pain. He will heal you. He will guide you as you reaffirm yourself without your loved one in the new life he has given you in Christ Jesus.

Prayer

Anoint my head with the oil of your healing, dear Lord. Beginning today, may I see myself as an individual created specially by you with a new future. Help me to trust your grace and promise to walk with me into a new life, one filled with your love and care—but also filled with the wonderful memories of past loves. I praise you for your love, which is transforming me into a new creature. May I live daily in the grace of your divine love. *Amen.*

Beauty
from
the Ashes

*You can look forward to
what the future may hold,
searching the landscape,
looking for signs of new
growth appearing after the
fire, envisioning the wealth
of opportunities that have
not yet been tapped.*

KNOWING HOW TO
GRIEVE INTENTIONALLY
is important when
attempting to recover
from your loss. Griev-
ing is not a passive
process. Rather, it is an
intentional and active
process that requires
time as you work
through the pain.
So warm yourself with
your memories, package

them for easy retrieval when you want to recall them, but also begin to realize you can store them as memories as well. Hold tight to the notion that you will get through this holiday or other special occasion.

You can have hope. Believe that you will not always feel this way, stricken with grief and aching for your deceased loved one to reappear. Life can be good for you again.

Notice, we said *can*—because it doesn't just happen. People can get stuck in their grief—and they call what they are doing "loyalty" or "love." We call it misunderstanding, or merely existing.

Perhaps you saw the movie *Message in a Bottle*. Paul Newman, playing the character Drudge, says to his son, who is grieving the death of his wife, "Now you choose, choose between yesterday and tomorrow. Pick one. Stick with it—and I will shut up and leave you alone."

Choose between yesterday and tomorrow. Each of us can focus on only one direction at a time. Backward—past tense. Or forward—future tense. You can either look backward with eyes fixed on what used to be. Or you can look forward to what the future may hold, searching the landscape, looking for signs of new growth appearing after the fire, envisioning the wealth of opportunities that have not yet been tapped. Pick one direction—either yesterday or this present moment, which is the beginning of your new future. And stick with it. We can't control everything in our lives, but we can choose which direction we are going to face.

What does your future hold? If, like Scrooge, you could see Christmas future, what would you see? Can you see yourself on the other side of your grief? Do you know that with some time and hard work, you can move through this period in your life?

You will not always be in pain. Maybe you have already experienced moments of feeling better, a little happier. Holidays may temporarily jolt you back into more pain, but this is normal and happens frequently while grieving.

Flowers are growing again in Yellowstone. The fire couldn't kill all life in that place. You too are alive, even though you've journeyed through the firestorm of death. Don't let your loved one's death kill your spirit. You can experience hope and promise of new growth. Remind yourself that you are a valuable person who may have a good part of life's journey ahead.

Regardless of your age, look around you with eyes wide open to see who else may be in your life right now who cares significantly for you and wants a relationship with you. It may be a son or daughter, a parent, a spouse, a brother or sister. Perhaps you have special friends or a cousin who is especially close to you. Find a way to appreciate and embrace them—perhaps in new ways.

Or perhaps your life is rather empty right now. You may recognize the desire for new friends, a need to make new acquaintances. Reaching out may be difficult, but this is a step in a healthy direction. You can begin again. Start with small steps.

You do have a future, with more joy ahead. Holidays and special days can feel joyful and fulfilling again. Challenge yourself to look ahead. What would you like to do or to have in your life? How do you want to live and create special times laden with meaning for yourself? You will learn so much about life and your relationships by the time you journey to the other side of grief. The journey may be painful. But the choice is pretty simple: Either stay with your painful emotions or work through them to rebuild your life.

One significant portion of your life may have ended with the death of your loved one. One volume of the book of your life has closed. But another volume is waiting to be written. You didn't ask for this. You likely did not want it. But now that it has happened, use this as an occasion to grow, to change, to become stronger and wiser. Life can be exciting, energizing, and even fulfilling after grief.

Grief changes us; hopefully it can change you for the better—make you more insightful, more understanding of what life is all about and what is important to you. *Message in a Bottle* ends with the idea that losing a significant person through death helps us better understand the meaning of life. As the movie ends, you hear these words: "If some lives form a perfect circle, others take shape in ways we cannot predict or always understand. Loss has been a part of my journey, but it has also shown me what is precious. So has a love for which I can only be grateful."

Take hold of your life. Believe your life is not over. You still have reasons for being here. Begin to find out what those reasons are.

Action

Healthy Behaviors

> As you move through the grief process, you will be able to see yourself as having a life independent of your deceased loved one. Take this opportunity to discover who you are as a person. Invest yourself in this new phase of life.

Here are some things you can do to begin to invest in a new phase of life.

- You may have felt that you were doing well prior to a particular holiday. Having a resurgence of grief on a holiday is normal, even if the death happened two or three years ago. Because everyone is different, you cannot put a timetable on grief. You may have been in shock longer than others or avoided dealing with your grief earlier in the process. If your loved one died more than three years ago, however, and your grief is still sharp and painful, think seriously about receiving grief counseling. The intensity and frequency of grief should diminish over the first few years, and if this hasn't happened, you may be holding on to some things that are preventing you from moving on in your life. Though holidays and special days can eventually become filled with joy once again, some people need additional help in reaching that point. Try not to view that as a weakness. Seeking additional help is a sign of courage and will likely result in positive benefits for you.

- Try to recognize purposely how your deceased loved one influenced who you are today. Determine what you learned from your relationship with this special person. You are obviously a different person from who you would have been without that relationship, but those benefits are not lost or gone now that your loved one is dead. Carry that uniqueness with you into the future.

- Move to embrace this new volume of your life. You will die some day, but in the meantime, you have a choice. You can either live your life handicapped by your grief, or you can deal effectively with your grief to embrace life again. We recommend you choose to live life to the fullest. You will undoubtedly see new gifts and blessings as you move along your life's journey.

- Write a list of goals, desires, and hopes that you have for your life from this point on, especially as they apply to the holidays and other special days in your life. Decide how you would like them to become an important part of your new life so they may enhance your present and future.

R e f l e c t i o n

Christian Meditation

"For I know the plans I have for you," declares the LORD, "plans to prosper you and not to harm you, plans to give you hope and a future."

Jeremiah 29:11

The LORD will fulfill his purpose for me;
your love, O LORD, endures forever—
do not abandon the works of your hands.

Psalm 138:8

Obviously you did not cause the death of your loved one. This tragedy happened against your will, and you were the recipient of all the pain and grief that comes with death. You were not responsible for it, and as Christians we also believe that God does not *cause* death. But he does *allow* it to happen. It is part of our brokenness as human beings in this world. Death is the curse and consequence of sin.

At the same time, what happens in our lives does not happen by chance. God is in ultimate control and will work things together for our good. Sometimes that good doesn't come as quickly as we would like. Sometimes we have to wait a long time before we can even begin to see the good. But we believe that God has a purpose, a goal, in mind for us, for God is intricately involved in our lives. There is a reason why we are here—and there is a reason that is uniquely yours, alone, individually. The death of someone we love often calls into question this conviction.

We do a lot of our living jointly with others. We plan trips together as a family. Spouses nurture shared dreams of retirement or visions of what they might do together as they progress through various phases of life. Parents have dreams and hopes for their children—ambitions for their future career, marriage, and offspring. Children plan on their parents being around for protection, role modeling, unconditional love, and support. Siblings want a relationship that will last for life and in which they can share their mutual stories and the responsibility of caring for aging parents.

But death ends these relationships. Dreams, visions, goals, and joint ambitions are suddenly cut off. The future is pruned from the family tree—or at least it may seem so in your grief.

Basic questions begin to fly at you. Who am I (without my child, sibling, parent, or spouse)? What am I going to do now (now that I feel "all alone")?

You face a rather simple alternative at this point in your life. You can erroneously decide that a significant part of yourself died when your loved one died. Or you can acknowledge the death of this dear person but then work toward recognizing that you did not die. You still have a purpose for living.

The passages quoted at the beginning of this meditation underscore that God has a special purpose in mind for you. That purpose may now take a new, or different, shape. You are in fact moving into another phase of your life. Your life did not end with the death of your loved one, nor have you lost the reason for your continued existence on this earth. God may have something else in mind for you. God still has a reason for you to be here. A good reason. A productive reason.

So who are you? What is your purpose? Giving you a specific answer to these questions is, of course, impossible. Part of your grief journey is to determine your own answers. But remember that the Bible reminds us, "The LORD will fulfill his purpose for me; your love, O LORD, endures forever—do not abandon the works of your hands" (Ps. 138:8). Contained in this short passage is both a *promise* and a *prayer.*

The *promise* is that God has a purpose for you. You are his child, his servant, his ambassador. At the very least, the apostle Paul points out that as we receive comfort and encouragement from God, then "we can comfort those in any trouble with the comfort we ourselves have received from God" (2 Cor. 1:4).

The *prayer* is that God will not leave you alone. God will not abandon you, even though you may feel that way at the present moment. He holds you in the palm of his hand. Whenever it seems that he is distant from us, we are probably the ones who have moved away.

In order to recognize that God has not abandoned you, you need to look again in God's direction (not toward the grave). Your purpose for being here goes well beyond your relationship with the deceased. The person you loved, the person who has died, was not the only important person in your life. You most likely have many other relationships. You have or will have many other involvements. Each of these relationships is also part of God's plan for you.

Finding a proper balance between recognizing and accepting the fact that you are an important individual while at the same time being part of a broader social system can be tricky. In some ways it is like being a member of a sports team. Imagine you are an important player on the team. You have your own special position to play. The rest of the team counts on your energy, skill, and presence of mind to help win the game. Then one day a talented team member is injured and cannot play. The coach may move you to a different position, requiring you and the team to make adjustments. The game doesn't stop, though the team probably feels differently now that the injured person is missing. But the game goes on.

In many ways, God has organized our life of faith in the same way. Consider Hebrews 11. You will find a list of the heroes of faith, individuals who fought valiantly for the cause of God. And then they died. But the cause went on. Others took up the challenge. But notice how the chapter ends. "God had planned something better for us so that only together with us would they be made perfect" (Heb. 11:40). Christians have individual *and* group purposes.

Life is like a relay race. Your loved one has run his or her lap. He or she has handed the baton to you. You are still in the race. You still have a purpose, and failing to pursue that purpose lets the rest of the team down. Hebrews 12 reminds us that we are "surrounded by such a great cloud of witnesses" so that we are encouraged to "fix our eyes on Jesus . . . so that [we] will not grow weary and lose heart" (vv. 1–3).

The baton is now in your hand. The race is still yours to run. God has a purpose for you—a purpose that goes far beyond what he was able to do through your relationship with your deceased loved one.

As you read the following verse again, let God speak to you through the words of Jeremiah: "For I know the plans I have for you," declares the LORD, "plans to prosper you and not to harm you, plans to give you hope and a future" (Jer. 29:11). Follow God's leading and together with him walk into the future by living fully in the present. He does not have plans to harm you. He wants you to prosper. Believe that. You will get through your grief and be granted a fulfilling future.

Prayer

Help me to fashion a new beginning here on earth, Lord, for I have not died. May I have the courage and patience to follow you, to keep my eyes on you, to know that you will again fill my life with good things, that you will bring beauty from the ashes. You are full of grace and peace. May I sense that grace and peace as I move into tomorrow. *Amen.*

Appendix

A Candle Lighting Memorial for Those Who Are Grieving

AN IMPORTANT PART OF THE GRIEF PROCESS is to pay tribute to and remember on this special occasion the one who has died. This memorial tribute is designed for use with four candles, arranged either in a circle or in some other manner in keeping with your own personal taste. The tribute can be used alone by an individual or in a small family setting. When used alone, feel free to change the pronouns from plural ("we") to singular ("I").

As we light these candles, we remember _____ _____ (name of deceased), who was important to us. On special occasions and holidays past, you created a wealth of memories with us. We are mindful that a significant change has occurred

83

with your death. You were so special to us, and now you are no longer here. How we wish you could return. We feel an empty place in our hearts and lives that had been filled with your presence. Now we grieve for all that had been—all that used to be with you—and all that we did not want to end. The harsh reality that you will never again share a holiday or this special occasion with us is painful to acknowledge. We agonize and grieve for you. We know in doing this that we will slowly heal. But we will never forget you or how you enhanced our lives and contributed to what we have become because of you. Therefore, these four candles honor your presence on this earth. We light one for our love for you, another for our memories of holidays or special days past, another for our grief in the present, and one for our hope for the future.

As we light this first candle, we are warmed by our love for you and the love we shared together. You hold a treasured place in our hearts and minds as a person we laughed with, shared deep meaningful thoughts and feelings with, argued with, perhaps at times were angry with, and yet someone we could reconnect with and feel close to. You gave us joy in the relationships we shared with you. Thank you for sharing your life with us.

This second candle represents our memories of holidays or special days past—the traditions we created together, the things you did to add to the uniqueness of the day. We thank you for the gift your life brought to our lives. We created meaning for the holidays and special days together. Now that you are dead, the traditions will never be quite the same. There remains an unfilled place—an empty chair—because you are no longer with us. We need to say good-bye to the possibility of things being the same and recognize that with your death our lives will be different. Thank you for contributing to our wonderful memories of meaningful holiday celebrations.

We now light the third candle, which represents the grief we experience as we contemplate living the rest of our lives without you. We treasure the fond memories, but we understand that we no longer have a relationship with you beyond those memories. You have left this world, and we are left in this world without you. We resolve to find ourselves complete in and of ourselves. You are in a better place; we will make *this* place better for ourselves. We will find the courage to persevere in the work of grieving so that we can confront our sorrow and move through the pain to the other side of grief.

The fourth and final candle we light signifies our hope for the future. We resolve to start again—to feel new life surging through our hearts. We will go through the fire and the pain, but eventually our mourning can turn to dancing. There will be a new beginning, the start of a new volume in our lives. This new beginning may be muted and unclear right now, but with work and trust and hope, the sun will again be bright.

For you, _____ (name of the deceased), the person who graced our lives for a time, and for our hope for the lives ahead of us, we light these four candles in your honor and with our hope.

A Candle Lighting Memorial for Christians Who Are Grieving

An important part of the grief process is to pay tribute to and remember on this special occasion the one who has died. This memorial tribute is designed for use with four candles, arranged either in a circle or in some other manner in keeping with your own personal taste. The tribute can be used alone by an individual or in a small family setting. When used alone, feel free to change the pronouns from plural ("we") to singular ("I").

As we light these candles, we remember _____ (name of deceased), who was important to us. On special occasions and holidays past, you created a wealth of memories with us. We are mindful that a significant change has occurred with your death. You were so special to us, and now you are no longer here. How we wish you could return. We feel an empty place in our hearts and lives that had been filled with your presence. Now we grieve all that had been—all that used to be with you—and all that we did not want to end. The harsh reality that you will never again share a holiday or special day with us is painful to acknowledge. We agonize and grieve for you, with the prayer that God will give us the strength to bear this burden. We know in doing this that God will slowly heal us. But we will never forget you or how you enhanced our lives and contributed to what we have become because of you. Therefore, these four candles honor your presence on this earth. We light one for our love for you, another for our memories of holidays or special days past, another for our grief in the present, and one for our hope for the future.

As we light this first candle, we are warmed by our love for you and the love we shared together. You were God's gift to us, and you hold a treasured place in our hearts and minds as a person we laughed with, shared deep meaningful thoughts and feelings with, argued with, and perhaps at times were angry with. Yet you were someone we could reconnect with and feel close to. You gave us joy in the relationships we shared with you. Thank you for sharing your life with us.

This second candle represents our memories of holidays or special days past—the traditions we created together, the things you did to add to the uniqueness of the day. God gave us his greatest gift in his Son, Jesus Christ. And he gave us you. We thank you for the gift your life brought to our lives. Together we created meaning for the holidays and special days. Now that you are dead, the traditions will never be quite the same. There remains an unfilled place—an empty chair—because you are no longer with us. We need to say good-bye to the possibility of things being the same and recognize that with your death our lives will be different. Thank you for giving us wonderful memories of meaningful holiday and special day celebrations.

We now light the third candle, which represents the grief we experience as we contemplate living the rest of our lives without you. We treasure the fond memories, but we understand that we no longer have a relationship with you beyond those memories. You have left this world, and we are left in this world without you. We pray that God will help us to find ourselves complete in and of ourselves. You are in a better place; may God help us to make *this* place better for ourselves. May God grant us the courage to persevere in the work of grieving so that we can confront our sorrow and move through the pain to the other side of grief.

The fourth and final candle we light signifies our hope for the future. We know as Christians we have hope. We do grieve differently from those who have no hope, for we have Christ in our hearts, the one who has conquered death and the grave. Our hope is in God, who holds each of us in his tender care. He will go through the fire and pain with us, and he will eventually change our mourning into dancing. There will be a new beginning, the start of a new volume in our lives. We have loved deeply. With God's help, we will be ready to begin to live again.

For you, _____ (name of deceased), who graced our lives for a time, for our hope for the lives ahead of us, and for our trust in the power of God to strengthen us, we light these four candles in your honor and with our eternal hope.

Notes

Preface

1. Susan J. Zonnebelt-Smeenge and Robert C. De Vries, *Getting to the Other Side of Grief: Overcoming the Loss of a Spouse* (Grand Rapids: Baker, 1998).

Chapter 1: The Firestorm

1. The acronym DEER was first suggested to us by Billie Humphrey, Aftercare Coordinator, K. L. Brown Funeral Home and Crematory, Jacksonville, Alabama.

2. C. S. Lewis, *A Grief Observed* (Greenwich, Conn.: Seabury Press, 1963), 7.

Chapter 4: Planting the Seeds for New Life

1. Lewis, *A Grief Observed,* 49.

Susan J. Zonnebelt-Smeenge is a clinical psychologist at Pine Rest Mental Health Services, Grand Rapids, Michigan. Her responsibilities include individual, marital, and family psychotherapy; psychological testing; supervision of interns and nonlicensed clinical staff; and clinical coordinator of psychotherapy services at Spectrum Health, Grand Rapids. She is a licensed psychologist, certified social worker, and registered nurse. She graduated from Aquinas College and Mercy Central School of Nursing in Grand Rapids and completed advanced studies at Western Michigan University (Ed.D. and M.A. in counseling psychology).

Robert C. De Vries is professor of church education and director of M.A. programs at Calvin Theological Seminary, Grand Rapids, Michigan. He is an ordained pastor in the Christian Reformed Church. He is published in journals and magazines and writes for CRC Publications. He's a graduate of Calvin College and Calvin Theological Seminary, and his advanced degrees include a Ph.D. in adult education from Michigan State University and a D.Min. in church administration from McCormick Theological Seminary, Chicago.

Both authors regularly conduct workshops and speak on grief issues.